Let's Celebrate!
Special Days Around the World

Author's Note

There are so many celebrations and traditions in the world — more than one person could experience in an entire lifetime, and far more than one book can contain. Not everyone from a culture or a faith observes the same traditions or celebrates the same special days. Some traditions span many countries and cultures. There's a big world beyond this book.

As you read, ask yourself what each special day has in common with the others in the book. How many connections can you find?

Thank you for coming to the celebration!
— Kate DePalma

Pronunciation Guide & Settings

Kodomo no Hi *(koh-DOH-mo NO HEE)* in Japan

Spring Festival *(SPRING FES-teh-val)* in China

Matariki *(mah-tah-REE-kee)* in New Zealand

Inti Raymi *(IN-tee RAY-mee)* in Peru

Carnaval *(car-nah-VAL)* in Brazil

Midsommar *(MISS-sum-mar)* in Sweden

Nowruz *(no-ROOZ)* in Iran

Passover *(PASS-oh-ver)* in the United States

New Yam Festival *(NOO YAM FES-teh-val)* in Nigeria

Novy God *(NO-vee GODT)* in Russia

Eid al-Fitr *(EED al-FIT-ur)* in Egypt

Día de Muertos *(DEE-ah DEH MWER-tos)* in Mexico

Diwali *(deh-VAH-lee)* in India

Acknowledgments

The author would like to thank the many people who helped ensure the accuracy of this book, including:

Autumn Allen • Li Chen • Kara Dentice • Elina DeVos • Hoda Elsharkawi • Ruoqing Fu • Naoko Komiya • Dr. Rangi Matamua
Ben Milam • Ayaka Mizoe • Leo Montenegro • Tomoyo Nagase • Bruno Olsson • Gabriela Quinte • Lisa Rosinsky • Dr. Melody Ann Ross
Akash Sahoo • Sarahy Sigie • Homa Sabet Tavangar • Stephanie Thomas • Mark Agu Uche • Stefanie Paige Wieder

Barefoot Books, 23 Bradford Street, 2nd Floor, Concord, MA 01742
Barefoot Books, 29/30 Fitzroy Square, London, W1T 6LQ

Text copyright © 2019 by Kate DePalma. Illustrations copyright © 2019 by Martina Peluso
The moral rights of Kate DePalma and Martina Peluso have been asserted

First published in United States of America by Barefoot Books, Inc
and in Great Britain by Barefoot Books, Ltd in 2019. All rights reserved

Graphic design by Sarah Soldano, Barefoot Books. Art directed by Kate DePalma
Educational notes by Stephanie Thomas and Kate DePalma
Reproduction by Bright Arts, Hong Kong. Printed in China on 100% acid-free paper

This book was typeset in Adobe Garamond Pro, Bembo Infant and Exquise
The illustrations were prepared in acrylics, pastels and pencil with digital embellishments

Hardback ISBN 978-1-78285-833-1 • Paperback ISBN 978-1-78285-834-8
E-book ISBN 978-1-78285-937-6

British Cataloguing-in-Publication Data: a catalogue record for this book
is available from the British Library

Library of Congress Cataloging-in-Publication Data
is available under LCCN 2019024622

Let's Celebrate!

Special Days Around the World

written by **Kate DePalma**

illustrated by **Martina Peluso**

Barefoot Books
Step inside a story

Let's bake some treats!

Let's light the lights!

We just can't wait for fun days
and bright nights.

On Kodomo no Hi*, we get quite a treat.

We unwrap oak leaves and find rice cakes to eat!

*Pronounced *koh-DOH-mo NO HEE*

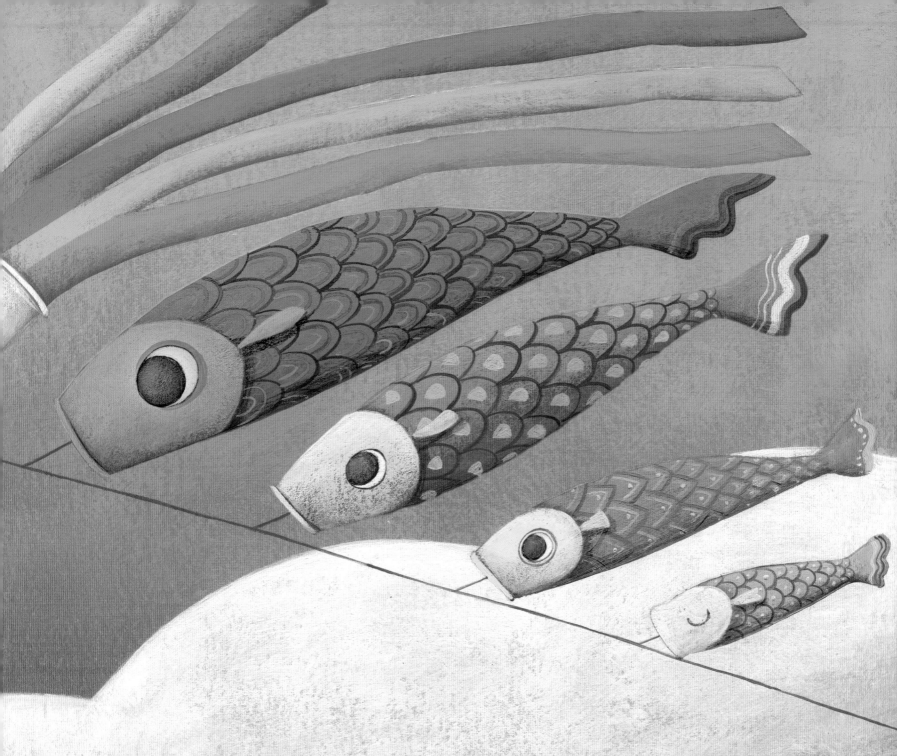

The fish flags we hang represent family —
My father, my mother, my brother and me!

Bright new year lanterns we hang up outdoors
Wish us happy Spring Festival* — good luck galore!

*Pronounced SPRING FES-teh-val

Midnight arrives. The fireworks begin
To chase away winter and let springtime in.

We reach Matariki* when nine bright stars rise.

We gather by firelight, eyes on the skies.

*Pronounced mah-tah-REE-kee

It's an earth-oven feast when the dawn light appears.
We let go of loved ones we've lost the last year.

Today's Inti Raymi*! The shell's trumpet blast
Tells the crowd to be quiet — the king's going past!

*Pronounced *IN-tee RAY-mee*

He's costumed in gold and a rainbow of shades.
We give thanks for the sun on the year's shortest day.

Carnaval* night brings quite the display.
Our crowns burst with feathers as sequined backs sway. *Pronounced *car-nah-VAL*

The streets fill with samba. Parade floats roll by

As dozens of dancers reach up to the sky.

Midsommar's* here! Bring flowers and greens.

We'll dance and make crowns like we're all kings and queens.

*Pronounced *MISS-sum-mar*

On this warm summer solstice when day stretches long

It's fun to make merry with picnics and song.

Our lush Nowruz* table is covered in dishes,
With bean sprouts and flowers and apples and fishes.

*Pronounced no-ROOZ

We all crowd around it to welcome the spring
Giving thanks for the fresh start that each new year brings.

We clean out our kitchen and sweep up the crumbs,
Then gather at sundown when Passover* comes.

*Pronounced *PASS-oh-ver*

Why is this night different? Our big seder meal
Shows that we're glad for the freedom we feel.

It's New Yam Festival*! Harvest is done.
We share all the yams. The king gets the first one.

*Pronounced NOO YAM FES-teh-val

Piling dishes with yams so high they might fall,
We could eat them all night and not finish them all!

Novy God* falls in winter and marks the new year.
We welcome midnight sharing food and good cheer.

*Pronounced NO-vee GODT

We open our gifts, the tree twinkling above.
We say "S novim godom*!" to those that we love.
*Pronounced *SNOW-veem go-DOME*

Today's Eid al-Fitr* — blow up the balloons!
Ramadan's at an end when we spot the new moon.

*Pronounced EED al-FIT-ur

We say "Eid Mubarak*!" to friends after prayers.
Then the smells of a great three-day feast fill the air.

*Pronounced *EED moo-BAH-rak*

On Día de Muertos*, the day of the dead,
We make altars with gifts — orange flowers and bread.

*Pronounced DEE-ah DEH MWER-tos

Warm candle glow fills the graveyards with light.
We pray that our loved ones return for the night.

Night shines like day when Diwali* dusk falls
And we toast the idea that good conquers all.

*Pronounced *deh-VAH-lee*

We light tiny oil lamps — each one a small spark.
When we gather, the light overpowers the dark.

When it's time to celebrate, we know the way.

We can all come together, no matter the day.

Calendar of Special Days

JANUARY	FEBRUARY	MARCH	APRIL	MAY	JUNE	JULY	AUGUST	SEPTEMBER	OCTOBER	NOVEMBER	DECEMBER

Passover
March or April*

Spring Festival
January or February*

Nowruz
March to April*

Kodomo no Hi
May 5

Matariki
June or July*

New Yam Festival
August, September or October

Diwali
October or November*

Carnaval
February or March

Midsommar
June

Inti Raymi
June 24

Día de Muertos
October 31 – November 2

Novy God
December 31 – January 7

Eid al-Fitr
Varies**

*The timing of some special days (marked here with a *) is based on calendars that don't measure time in the same way the year is measured on the timeline above. For example, China uses a lunar calendar (based on the movements of the moon), but the calendar on this timeline is solar (based on the movements of the sun). That's why Spring Festival falls in January some years, and other years it falls in February.

**Every year, the date of Eid al-Fitr falls about 11 days earlier on the calendar used for this timeline.

Kodomo no Hi in Japan

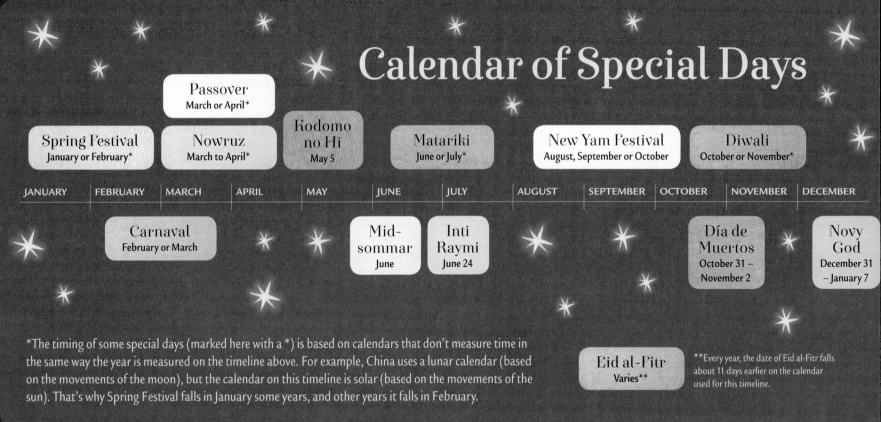

- **Kodomo no Hi** *(koh-DOH-mo NO HEE)*, or Children's Day, has celebrated the strength, health and happiness of children in Japan for over a thousand years. Its origins are from a festival known as Boy's Day. It falls on the fifth day of the fifth month — May 5.

- Bright **koi** *(KOY)* fish flags called **koinobori** *(koy-noh-BORE-ee)* are hung outside the home. Koinobori are a symbol of strength and persistence from an ancient legend. Each fish represents a family member: The black **magoi** *(MAG-oy)* is for a father, the red **higoi** *(HIG-oy)* is for a mother, and the smallest fish represent children. At the top vibrant streamers fly, sometimes with a family crest.

- Families decorate inside with miniature samurai figures called **yoroi** *(YO-roy)* and children wear paper **kabuto** *(kah-BOO-toe)* helmets as another symbol of strength.

- On Children's Day treats called **kashiwa mochi** *(kah-SHE-wah MOE-chee)* are shared. These rice cakes are filled with sweet bean paste and wrapped in oak (kashiwa) leaves.

Spring Festival in China

- Spring Festival (**Chūn Jié** *[CHUN gee-EH]* in Mandarin) in China celebrates the first day of the Chinese lunar calendar, typically in January or February. The celebrating lasts a whole week!

- During Spring Festival there are parades and celebrations in the streets, with lots of lanterns and a great big dragon held high above the crowds.

- To prepare, everyone helps clean, shop and decorate. Sweeping away last year's dust and wearing new clothes welcomes good fortune in the new year.

- Red lanterns are hung, along with poems and wishes of luck written on scrolls.

- Families share large meals together, eating dishes like fish, dumplings and rice balls filled with bean paste or minced meat called **yuanxiao** *(yoo-an-she-OW)* and **tangyuan** *(TAHN-yoo-an)*.

- Fireworks ward off the mythological **Nian** *(nee-AN)* monster, who is afraid of loud noises and anything red. This is why all of the decorations for Spring Festival are bright red!

- As a special treat, children eat candied hawthorn fruits. Elders give money to children in red envelopes, called **hongbao** *(hong-BOW)*, for good health and happiness.

"Good luck!"

"Happy Spring Festival!"

Matariki in New Zealand

- Around June or July every year, the **Maōri** *(may-ORE-ee)* people of New Zealand celebrate when they first see the star cluster named after the goddess **Matariki** *(mah-tah-REE-kee)* appear in the night sky.

- Each of the nine stars in the Matariki cluster has a meaning related to a natural force, like saltwater, winds or animals. Early on the day of Matariki when it is still dark outside, people gather to examine the stars to predict what will happen in the year to come. For example, if the star that represents food that comes from the earth, **Tupuānuku** *(too-poo-AH-noo-koo)*, looks bright, a bountiful harvest is predicted.

- Sacred words are spoken to ask the goddess Matariki to guide loved ones who have died since the last Matariki celebration into the afterlife.

- Food cooks in an earth oven called a **hāngī** *(HANG-ee)* in Maōri. A hāngī is made by heating stones in the bottom of a pit with a fire. When the stones are hot, food wrapped in flax leaves or wet cloth is placed on top of the stones, and then the whole thing is covered in earth, which traps the heat and cooks the food. When the food is taken out, steam rises into the sky as an offering to the stars. Then everyone enjoys a dawn feast.

Inti Raymi in Peru

- **Inti Raymi** *(IN-tee RAY-mee)* falls on June 24. In the **Quechua** *(KETCH-ooh-wah)* language, Inti Raymi means "Sun Festival."

- Cities throughout South and Central America celebrate Inti Raymi, but the largest gathering is a dramatic performance of the traditional Inca ceremony by indigenous actors in Cusco, Peru.

- At the **Coricancha** *(core-ee-CON-cha)*, the Temple of the Sun in Cusco, a large seashell called a **pututo** *(poo-TOO-toe)* is played, silencing the crowds for the **Inca** *(EEN-kah)*, the king.

- The Inca addresses the sun at the main plaza outside the temple. He thanks the sun for blessing the people. With his queen, the **Qoya** *(KOY-ah)*, he leads the parade through the streets of Cusco to the fortress **Sacsayhuaman** *(sack-sye-WHAH-man)*. The Inca and Qoya are carried on golden thrones.

- Thousands of people gather at Sacsayhuaman to watch. The Inca praises the sun and gives a speech. Then musicians and performers praise Inti, the god of the sun.

- Inti Raymi is also observed by indigenous peoples in towns in Peru, Ecuador and beyond. People don bright costumes to enjoy music and food together in praise of the sun.

Carnaval in Brazil

- **Carnaval** *(car-nah-VAL)* is the season of parades and parties that takes place every February or March in Brazil. This celebration is the last day of food and fun before Lent, a solemn season of forty days in the Christian calendar often marked by fasting (not eating at specific times).

- The costumes worn for Carnaval parades use eye-catching feathers and sequins to stand out in a sea of vibrant outfits.

- Parade floats for Carnaval can sometimes be three stories high!

- Carnaval parades move to the beat of samba. Samba is an energetic, rhythmic Brazilian music and dance style that has roots in West African traditions.

- Samba schools (or **escolas de samba** *[es-COLE-as deh SAHM-bah]* in Portuguese) are schools for drummers, dancers and performers to learn samba. School groups spend almost the entire year preparing for Carnaval. The groups compete with one another during the parades, dancing for the gathered crowds and a panel of judges. They are graded on costumes, music and the theme of their dance.

Midsommar in Sweden

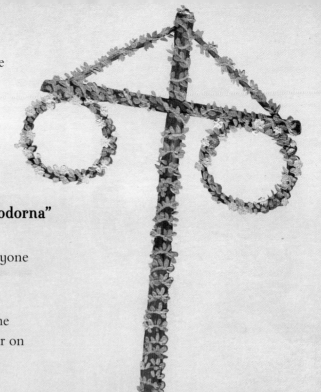

- **Midsommar** *(MISS-sum-mar)* is celebrated in Sweden in late June on the eve of the summer solstice.

- Summer solstice is the longest day of the year. People travel from towns and cities to the countryside to celebrate Midsommar.

- People enjoy singing and folk dancing around a maypole called a **midsommarstång** *(MISS-sum-mars-tong)*. The maypole is decorated with greenery and flowers.

- One popular Midsommar dance done around the pole is called **"Små grodorna"** *(SMAH GRO-dor-na)* or "The Little Frogs."

- Picnics include herring, boiled new potatoes and other special foods. Everyone enjoys summer's first local strawberries with cream for dessert. Swedish strawberries are very small and sweet!

- People decorate homes with things that grow only in summertime — some believe those plants to have special powers. The flower crowns people wear on Midsommar are said to bring love and good health all year long.

Nowruz in Iran

- **Nowruz** *(no-ROOZ)* is a Persian festival celebrated in Iran and around the world by people of many faiths.

- Nowruz begins in March on the Vernal Equinox, when spring begins. It is about new beginnings — cleaning away the past year and starting fresh.

- People clean their homes, wear new clothes and create a **Haft Seen** *(HAFT SEEN)* table. "Haft Seen" means "seven Ss," because the seven traditional items for the table start with the letter "s" in Persian. But the Haft Seen table often has more than seven items.

- The table includes items like sprouts, apples, garlic, vinegar, coins, hyacinth and a red spice called **sumac** *(SOO-mac)* to represent ideas like life's sweetness and bitterness, wealth and health.

- Families gather, often at the home of the oldest family member as a sign of respect, and celebrate the moment of the spring equinox.

- For thirteen days, people enjoy dinners and reflect on the year ahead.

- On the last day, those celebrating take the sprouts from the Haft Seen to the closest river or stream and allow them to float away, letting go of the old and welcoming the new year.

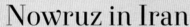

Passover in the United States

- **Passover** *(PASS-oh-ver)* (or **Pesach** *[PAY-sock]* in Hebrew) is a Jewish festival observed worldwide. It celebrates the Jewish people's freedom from enslavement in ancient Egypt.

- According to the story of Passover, God sent ten plagues to Egypt to try to convince the ruler of Egypt, the Pharaoh, to set the Jewish slaves free. Passover is named for God passing over the houses of Jews to protect them during the tenth plague.

- When the Jewish people eventually fled Egypt, they did not have time to wait for bread to rise. Because of this, during the eight days of Passover only unleavened bread (bread that has not risen) is eaten.

- Passover celebrations start with a service and meal called a **seder** *(SAY-der)* on the first and second nights.

- To prepare, the family gets rid of any leavened bread, cleans the house and sweeps crumbs away.

- Some people wear a **yarmulke** *(YAH-mah-kah)* or **kippah** *(KEE-pah)* — a small head covering worn as a sign of respect — and everyone usually dresses nicely.

- The seder follows the Passover story as it is read from a book called the **Haggadah** *(hah-GAH-dah)*.

- A decorative seder plate or **k'arah** *(CAR-ah)* holds symbolic items for the seder service.

New Yam Festival in Nigeria

- Festivals celebrating the yam harvest are observed throughout West Africa. One of the largest celebrations can be found among the **Igbo** *(EE-boo)* people of Nigeria. The festival is called **Iwa ji** *(IH-wah GEE)*, **Iri ji** *(EE-ree GEE)* or **Ike ji** *(EE-kay GEE)* in different dialects of the Igbo language.

- It takes place when yams are harvested, between August and October. They are the first crop harvested and their bounty lasts an entire year.

- The night before the festival, old yams are cast aside or eaten to make way for the fresh harvest.

- During New Yam Festival, the harvest is presented to the king or eldest member of the community. It is his job to offer the yams to God, the ancestors and the yam god. He thanks them for giving plenty to eat for the year.

- The king eats the first yam because it is believed that he is the in-between for the community and the gods.

- Then everyone eats together and celebrates with music and dancing.

Novy God in Russia

- **Novy God** *(NO-vee GODT)* is observed in Russia and beyond on December 31. Families often celebrate until January 7, when Russians observe Christmas.

- At one time, the Soviet government did not allow religious celebrations. Because people were unable to openly celebrate Christmas, they enjoyed their Christmas traditions on New Year's Eve instead. Today Novy God is celebrated by people of many faiths and backgrounds.

- Many of the symbols and decorations for Novy God resemble those for Christmas, though their roots are actually in Nordic and Slavic traditions.

- **Ded Moroz** *(DED more-OHZ)*, or Grandfather Frost, is said to bring gifts to children with help from his granddaughter **Snegurochka** *(sneh-gur-OACH-kah)*, the Snow Maiden.

- New year trees, called **yolka** *(YOLE-kah)*, are spruce or fir trees decorated with lights and ornaments and sometimes topped with a star. Decorative nutcracker figurines are also popular for Novy God.

- Families gather for a dinner of many courses and make wishes when the clock strikes midnight.

- To wish one another a good year, people say "**S Novim Godom**!" *(SNOW-veem go-DOME)*.

Eid al-Fitr in Egypt

- **Eid al-Fitr** *(EED al-FIT-ur)* celebrates the end of Ramadan, an important month in Islam. Muslims throughout the world observe this day.

- Ramadan is a holy month of fasting during the ninth month of the Islamic calendar. Muslims fast from dawn until dusk for thirty days to remember the first time the **Quran** *(kur-AHN)*, the central holy text of Islam, was revealed to the prophet Muhammad*.

- Eid al-Fitr means "Festival of Breaking the Fast" in Arabic.

- People wear new clothes and share gifts with each other. It is also customary to be generous to those in need that day.

- It is a religious day with many prayers and traditions for families. Prayers are held in mosques and also outside with prayer rugs. In some places, like Egypt, balloons are released into the sky when prayers end.

- After prayers, families visit and might go to the cemetery to remember the dead.

- People greet each other with "**Eid Mubarak**!" *(EED moo-BAH-rak)*, which means "Have a blessed Eid!" in Arabic.

- The festival typically lasts for three days but celebrations can go on all week.

*Muslim readers might say "peace be upon him" after speaking the name of a prophet.

Día de Muertos in Mexico

- **Día de Muertos** *(DEE-ah DEH MWER-tos)* comes from the indigenous **Nahua** *(nah-HOO-ah)* cultures of Mexico, which include the Aztec people. In these cultures, the dead remain part of the community and it is thought to be important to remember them.

- In homes and cemeteries, **ofrendas** *(oh-FREN-dahs)*, or altars, are created to welcome spirits back to the land of the living.

- Ofrendas are covered in marigolds, whose bright orange shade is thought to guide souls back from the afterlife. Water, food, salt and a bread called **pan de muerto** *(PAN deh MWER-toe)* are left for the spirits after their long journey. There are candles for each relative who has died, along with photos and personal items. Burning incense is thought to clean the air and lift prayers into the sky.

- Small painted skull figurines called **calaveras** *(call-ah-VEH-ras)* are an important symbol of Día de Muertos. Decorated calaveras made of sugar are often given to children, and people dress up and paint their faces to resemble calaveras too.

- People hang carefully cut paper flag decorations called **papel picado** *(pah-PEL pee-CAH-doh,* Spanish for "pierced paper"). They represent the nature of life: beautiful and fragile.

Diwali in India

- **Diwali** *(deh-VAH-lee)* (or **Deepavali** *[dee-pah-VAH-lee]*) means "row of lights" in Sanskrit. It is a festival of lights enjoyed around the world, with the largest celebrations in India.

- Many religions celebrate their own form of Diwali including Hindu, Sikh, Jain and Buddhist faiths.

- Though there are many versions of the celebration, the common thread is the victory of good (light) over evil (dark).

- Diwali lasts for five days at the end of October or early November.

- On the first day, rows of candles or oil lamps called **diya** *(DEE-yah)* are set up. **Rangoli** *(ran-GO-lee)*, bright designs made of sand or rice flour, are also created at home. Rangoli bring good luck — patterns might be passed down and repeated for generations!

- The second day is for shopping and cooking.

- The third day is the darkest of the lunar calendar. Diya are lit to worship **Lakshmi** *(LUCK-shmee)*, the goddess of wealth, and bring light to the darkness.

- On the fourth day families share a meal called **Annakoot** *(ON-ah-koot)*, meaning "mountain of food."

- The final day, **Bhai Duj** *(BYE DOOJ)*, celebrates the bond between brothers and sisters.